Getting Ahead in Technology

Getting Ahead in Technology

Terry Cash

Illustrated by Helen Herbert

Longman

Longman Group UK Limited

Longman House
Burnt Mill, Harlow, Essex CM20 2JE, England
and Associated Companies throughout the World

First published 1990

British Library Cataloguing in Publication Data Cash, Terry
    Getting ahead in technology. – (Shared learning activities).
    1. Technology
    I. Title II. Herbert, Helen III. Series
    600
    ISBN 0-582-05869-4

Set in 11/12 Frutiger Light and Frutiger Bold

Produced by Longman Group (FE) Ltd
Printed in Hong Kong

Contents

Introduction

Our children live in an age of unprecedented change where technology aids and controls our lives more and more.

Tomorrow's world will belong to the scientist and the engineer. Technology embodies many of the skills and much of the knowledge of the sciences, but whereas science explores the world that is, technology is concerned with the creation of what will be.

Technology is now an important subject in every school's curriculum and an understanding of technology will be so important for our children who will work in a world that will become further and further dependent upon technological progress.

With step by step instructions, this book guides the reader through important activities that lay the foundation for a clearer understanding of technological processes and principles and, perhaps what is more important, it makes learning fun.

Many of the activities contain essential information which explains, clearly and simply, the technological processes involved and comprehensive lists of items required are provided. However, it is fully appreciated that expensive, specialised equipment is not easily obtainable which is why most of the experiments and investigation can be done with nothing more than items of household junk. In fact the only thing that is the needed is the sense of curiosity and inquisitiveness that every child has as a natural gift.

Air and flight

Flying machines

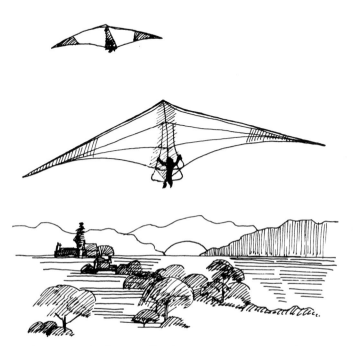

On the 17th December 1903, near Kitty Hawk which is in North Carolina in the United States, Orville Wright took off and flew in an aircraft powered by a small engine that he and his brother Wilbur had built. Its first flight was less than the wing span of a Jumbo jet, but it was the first heavier-than-air plane to take off and fly under its own power. The speed of development of flying machines was incredible. Only 16 years after the Wright brothers' 'Flyer' first took to the air, Alcock and Brown flew their 'Vickers Vimy' aircraft from Canada to Ireland across the Atlantic Ocean. By the end of the 1950's people were flying all over the world in jet powered airliners and less than 70 years after the first, hesitant hops into the air, Astronaut Neil Armstrong was walking on the moon.

Since people first walked on the Earth they have dreamed of flying like the birds. The earliest attempts at flying ended in injury or death and it wasn't until the mid 1800's that the first successful flights were made. Inventors had tried to copy the flapping of birds wings which proved almost impossible. It wasn't until people began to study skills of birds such as gulls that breakthroughs in flight were made. A gull uses the currents of air over the sea and cliffs to stay airborne for long periods without flapping its wings at all. This is called soaring. Intrepid flyers such as Percy Pilcher and Otto Lilienthal made flying machines that had fixed wings that glided through the air very much like hang gliders today.

Blow darts

To make your blow darts you will need two plastic drinking straws, one large one, such as the kind you get with drinks in a fast food restaurant, and a thinner straw that will fit inside the larger one. You will also need a post-card, scissors, a small blob of plasticine and some glue.

Cut two triangles, one large and one small, from thin card and glue them to the larger straw to make the wings and tail fin. Be patient and let the glue harden, then put a small blob of plasticine on the front of the dart so that it blocks the end of the straw.

To launch your dart, push the smaller straw inside the larger one and blow hard into the thin straw. The force of the air speeds the dart on its way. Experiment by changing the weight of plasticine to get a long, level flight. You can also try cutting flaps into the wings and fin to change the direction of flight. Happy landings!

Build a model hovercraft

A hovercraft 'flies' above the ground supported on a cushion of air made by a large, powerful fan. Part of the engine's power is also used to turn a propeller to push the hovercraft along.

A hovercraft is truly amphibious, moving over water just as easily as land. Hovercrafts usually have a rubber 'skirt' around the bottom which allows them to rise high enough off the ground to be able to glide over low obstacles. Hovercraft can be very fast and some are large enough to carry cars and passengers at over 80 kph (50 mph) across the sea.

To make a model hovercraft you will need two polystyrene ceiling tiles about 30 cm (12 in) square and tile cement or strong glue, such as Copydex. Polystyrene modelling cement for gluing plastic kits together will NOT stick tiles.

Cut a hole in the centre of one of the tiles about 15 cm (6 in) across using a sharp craft knife. Cut four strips of polystyrene about 2 cm (1 in) wide and 30 cm (12 in) long from the second tile and glue the strips round the edge of the first tile to make the 'skirt'. Finally cut

four more strips about 15 cm (6 in) long and 5 cm (2 in) wide and glue them around the central hole.

To 'fly' your hovercraft, put it on a smooth lino floor and ask an adult to help you blow air down through the hole using a powerful hairdrier. DON'T use the hairdrier on a polished table top because it could be scorched. The air rushing through the hole can only escape under the skirt of the hovercraft, lifting it fractionally off the ground. The model becomes almost weightless, held on its cushion of air, and it will skim across the floor with the gentlest touch, but only for as long as you keep blowing air through the central hole.

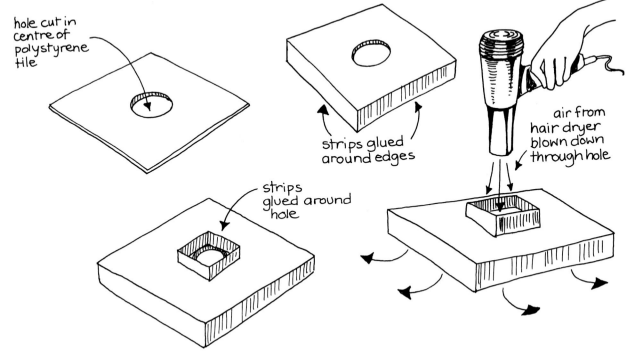

hole cut in centre of polystyrene tile

strips glued around edges

strips glued around hole

air from hair dryer blown down through hole

Balsa gliders

Balsa wood is extremely light, making it perfect for making flying machines which need to be as light as possible. You can buy balsa wood in any good model shop. You will need a sheet of thin balsa, about 1 mm (1/16th in) thick, and a stick of balsa about 30 cm (12 in) long, just over a centimetre (1/2 in) wide and 5 mm (1/4 in) thick. You will also need a sharp craft knife and a tube of balsa cement.

Gliders have long, thin wings that give them lots of lift, but you can design your own gliders with all kinds of wing shapes. Make a cutting plan for the balsa sheet like one of those shown and draw the outline onto the wood with a pencil or felt-tipped pen.

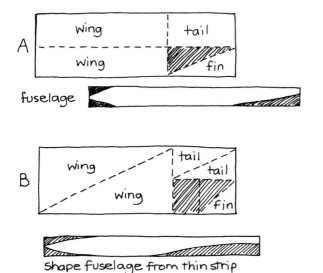

You may need to ask an adult to help you to carefully cut out the shapes with a sharp craft knife and use a cutting board NOT the table top!

Glue the wings, tail and fin to the balsa stick which will be the fuselage. You can shape the fuselage with sandpaper to make it an interesting shape. You will have to leave the glider overnight until the glue has completely dried and set hard.

Lastly, put a blob of plasticine on the nose of the plane so that it is just nose heavy when you hold it gently by the wing tips. Experiment by changing the weight until your glider flies straight and level. You can also buy balsa paint to make your model look even more exciting.

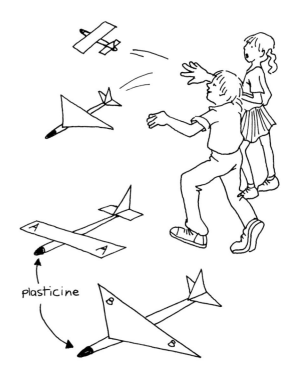

Nature's helicopters

Have you ever noticed on the ground under an ash or sycamore tree lots of little wing shaped seeds? These trees have evolved a way of dispersing their seeds using the wind. When the little ' helicopter' wings break free from the tree they spin rapidly in the wind and can be carried quite a long distance.

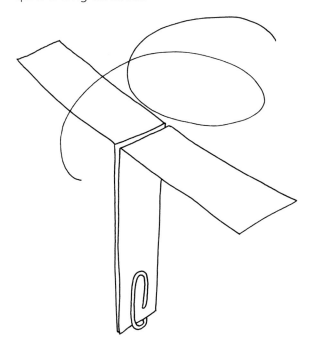

To discover how this happens take a piece of paper and cut a strip about 2 cm (1 in) wide and 30 cm. (12 in) long.

Fold the strip in half and fold down the 'wings' at either side as shown. Put a paper clip on the bottom to hold the strip in shape and act as the weight of the 'seed'. Drop the helicopter down some stairs or out of a window and watch it twirl in the air slowing its fall. Try changing the shape of the spinner. Do longer, wider wings carry the spinner further than shorter, thinner ones? What happens if you add more weight? Try it and see. Be careful if you are launching out of a window, you could fall a lot faster than your helicopter!

Flying Spinners

Another way to make a helicopter is to cut a propeller blade shape from a piece of card about 10 cm (4 in) long. Make a small hole in the centre of the propeller with the point of a pair of scissors and push a thin plastic straw (the kind that you get with small packet drinks) or a cocktail stick through the hole. Hold it in place with some sticky tape.

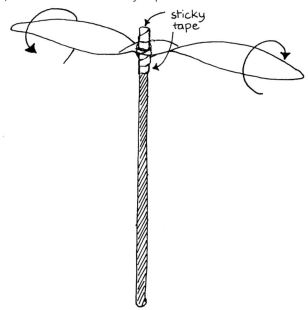

sticky tape

Twist the blades of the propeller as shown so that they push the air downwards and give lift.

To launch your spinner, hold the straw between your hands and rub one palm across the other. This will spin the propeller very fast and it should fly away. If it falls straight to the floor it may be that the spinning blades are pushing it down instead of lifting it up. You need to spin the propeller in the opposite direction then it should work.

Air pressure

Air does not seem to be particularly strong. Usually we hardly notice the air around us. Yet air, moving over the curved surface of an aeroplane's wings can lift it off the ground. A large airliner may weigh over 300 tonnes, but flies gracefully supported by the lifting force of the air. Moving air can also be very destructive. Sometimes we experience freak weather conditions that cause strong winds to blow. Hurricane force winds can uproot trees and blow the roofs from houses.

The air forms a thin, protective layer around the Earth. We call it the atmosphere. At very high levels, such as the tops of the highest mountains, there is so little air that it is very difficult to breathe. Aircraft must have air under pressure inside the cabins so that the passengers and crew can breathe normally. Down at lower levels the air presses down on everything, but we don't feel a weight pressing on our heads because the air pressure is all around us, pushing from all sides.

We use the strength of air in many ways. Take a look at a bicycle for example. Look at the tyres and think for a moment. What is actually holding up your weight? If you get a puncture letting the air out, the tyre goes flat. On big earthmovers the air in the massive tyres is holding up tons of earth.

You can feel the force of air under pressure with a bicycle pump. Hold your thumb tightly over the end of the pump and push the handle in. You will find it impossible to hold back the air as it gets squeezed inside the barrel of the pump and forces its way out past your thumb.

Magic plate lifter

You can use the strength of air to make a simple trick to fool your family and friends. All you need is a small balloon and a length of thin plastic tubing. Tape the neck of the balloon tightly around one end of the tube and put the balloon under a dinner plate on a table. Keep the tube hidden then ,when everyone sits down to tea, blow down the tube. The balloon will inflate a little and the plate will bob up. By blowing short puffs you can make the plate bob up and down in a very eerie and mysterious way.

You can also use your plate lifter to see who has the most puff. Place a book on the bag and blow hard. You should be able to lift the book easily. Repeat the test adding more books each time. How many books can you lift before you run out of puff?

Fire extinguisher

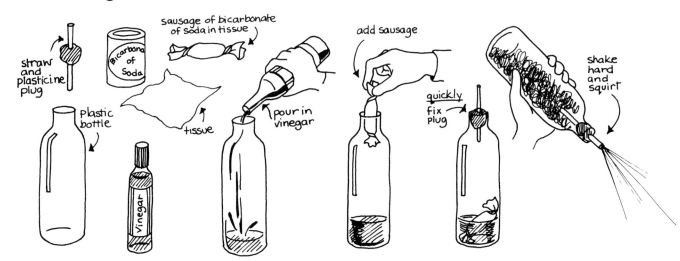

Many fire extinguishers work by mixing two chemicals together inside a strong, steel container. The chemicals produce masses of a gas called carbon dioxide and the pressure of the gas inside the container blows foam or water out of a nozzle that can be directed towards the fire. You can make a simpler version of a fire extinguisher using a plastic lemonade bottle.

Choose a small bottle, less than 1 litre if possible, and make a plug for the neck out of plasticine that has a wide drinking straw through the centre. When the plug is in place only about 2 cm (less than 1 inch) of the straw should stick down inside the bottle. Keep the plug to one side while you prepare the extinguisher. Pour vinegar into the bottle until it is about a third full. Next wrap baking soda (sodium bicarbonate) in tissue paper to make a long sausage that is narrow enough to be dropped easily through the neck of the bottle. A 'sausage' 15 cm (6 in) long containing several

tablespoonfuls of baking powder should be sufficient.

To operate your extinguisher take it outside where it cannot harm carpets or furniture. DON'T light a fire, this is only a demonstration model. With the plasticine and straw plug in one hand, drop the baking powder sausage through the neck of the bottle with the other and immediately push the plug firmly into the neck of the bottle.

Turn the bottle upside down, which will help to mix the contents, and direct the stream of foamy liquid into a bucket or down a drain. What happens is that the tissue paper rapidly soaks through and the baking powder is released into the vinegar. Vinegar is a weak acid which reacts with the sodium bicarbonate, giving off lots of carbon dioxide gas which makes the mixture froth up. The pressure of the gas builds up in the bottle and the only way that the pressure can be reduced is by pushing the liquid out of the bottle through the straw.

he magic of magnetism

People have known about magnetic force for hundreds of years. Sailors used chunks of magnetic rock called lodestone to help them navigate from one place to another. They had discovered that magnetic rock hung from a thread always pointed in the same direction, towards the North. Knowing where North was allowed them to set the right course for their home port.

Magnets are amazing, but a good one can be expensive and hard to find. Play magnets, sold in toy shops, are not very good for doing experiments with. They are usually made of plastic with tiny pieces of magnetised metal glued to the ends. If you can find a supplier who will sell you a good magnet ask for a set made from cobalt steel. Look after them and they will last for years, but remember that any magnet that is dropped or banged will lose its magnetism.

Test your magnets on as many different things as you can find. Try cups and saucers, glass jars and plastic bottles, aluminium pots and tin foil, keys, coins, rubber, brick and paper, knives and forks, wood, brass, paper clips and drawing pins.

Many things will not be attracted at all, but some things are attracted so well they will almost seem to jump at the magnet. Make a note of the things that are not attracted as well as those that are. What do you notice about all the things that 'stick' to your magnet?

Gone fishing

All you need is a large cardboard box which will be the fish tank, two thin garden canes about 40 cm (16 in) long, some string, cut-out paper fish shapes, two magnets and some paper clips.

Tie the magnets to the canes with a length of string to make two fishing rods. Push a paper clip on the nose of each of the fish. Make about ten fish in all. You can also decorate the side of the box to make it look like an aquarium. Put the fish in the tank and 'hook' them with your magnet. Don't peep into the tank, see how good you are at fishing.

You can make the game even more interesting by having simple maths questions on the side of each fish (perhaps multiplication tables) and you only keep a fish if you give the right answer to the sum.

Magnetic sailing ships

Sail your yachts under magnetic control and race your friends to port. Find some corks, cocktail sticks or tooth picks and some drawing pins. Ask an adult to help you cut each cork in half, lengthways with a sharp knife, push a drawing pin in the curved bottom and a cocktail stick in the flat top. Make a small sail with a square of paper and float your yacht in a shallow glass dish with about 1.5 cm (half an inch) of water in the bottom. Make three more yachts so that you and a friend can race two each.

cork

bar magnet

horseshoe magnet

cocktail sticks

drawing pins

thin card/ stiff paper

card sail

cocktail stick

cork

drawing pin

You will also need to make two magnetic rods. Tape or tie magnets to the ends of two sticks and raise the glass dish 5 cm (2 in) off the table by resting it on cotton reels, egg cups or books at each corner.

To sail the yachts you will have to move the magnets underneath the dish and attract the drawing pin in the bottom of one of your sailing ships. Gently move your magnetic wand and the ship will sail after it. What is so amazing is that the power of the magnet is able to pass through the glass and the water and still move the ship.

The contest can be decided by seeing who can move both of their ships from one end of the dish to the other in the fastest time.

Driving test

You can use a magnetic wand to drive a car round a race track. Get yourself a piece of stiff card about 40 cm (16 in) square, a magnet taped to a thin stick or garden cane and a piece cut from a wine bottle cork.

Draw a picture of a racing car on thin card about 3 cm (just over 1 inch) long. Draw it as though you are looking at the car from the side,

then cut round the outline with some scissors. Ask an adult to cut a slot in the top of a slice of cork with a sharp knife and wedge your racing car picture in the slot. Finally push a drawing pin in the bottom of the cork.

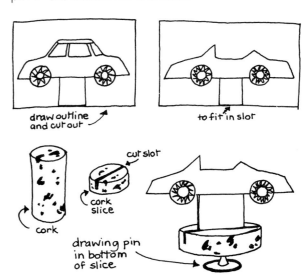

draw outline and cut out

to fit in slot

cut slot

cork slice

cork

drawing pin in bottom of slice

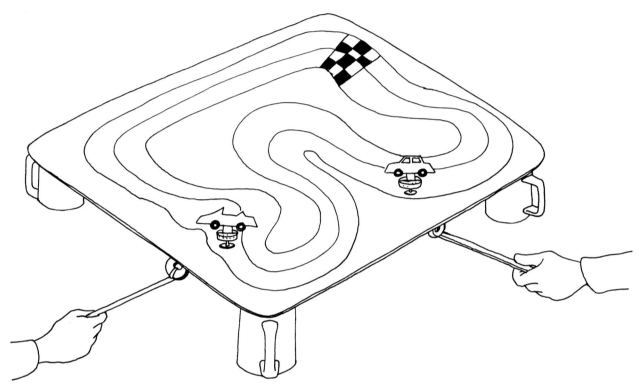

Use paint, pencils or felt-tipped pens to draw a race track on your square of card, don't forget a couple of hair-pin bends to really tax your driving skills and a long straight where you can pick up speed.

To drive your car place the race track on four upturned mugs, one at each corner, and steer your car round the track by moving your magnetic wand underneath the track. The car will turn and spin as it moves but with practice you will be able to steer it around all the twists and turns. Time your laps and race your friends.

Electro-magnets

An iron or steel rod can be magnetized with electricity. If you wrap the rod inside a coil of wire and pass an electric current through the wire, this causes little magnetic particles in the metal (called 'domains') to line up and turn it into a magnet.

Try it for yourself, it is very easy. All you need is a 4.5 volt battery, some thin wire (the best kind to get is bare wire that has no plastic insulation around it) and a large nail about 15 cm (6 in) long.

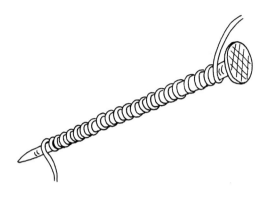

Spend some time carefully and patiently winding the wire around the nail in a tight coil. Start 2 cm (1 in) from one end of the nail and wrap the wire in neat coils around the nail until you get to within 2 cm of the other end. You can keep the coils in place by wrapping a little Sellotape around them as you go.

Finally connect the ends of the wire coil to the terminals of the battery. If you are using bare wire it is quite likely that it has a coat of lacquer on it which must be cleaned off first.

Rub 2 to 3 cm of each end of the wire with fine sandpaper to clean the ends and then connect up to the battery.

Put a simple switch in the circuit, like the ones described in the electricity section, so that you can turn your electromagnet on and off when you want.

Get a box of paper clips or drawing pins. Switch on your electro-magnet and dip the end of the nail into the box. The electricity flowing in the circuit magnetizes the nail which can then pick up the clips. You will be amazed at how strong a well-made electro-magnet can be. Large industrial electro-magnets can lift cars with ease.

Make your own electro-magnetic crane

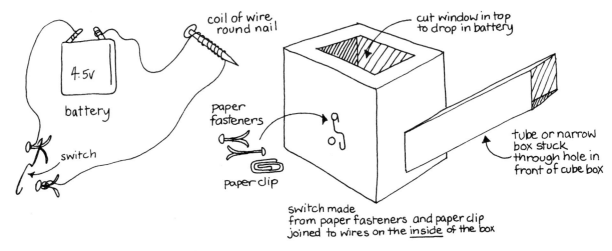

coil of wire round nail

4.5v

battery

switch

paper fasteners

paper clip

cut window in top to drop in battery

tube or narrow box stuck through hole in front of cube box

switch made from paper fasteners and paper clip joined to wires on the inside of the box

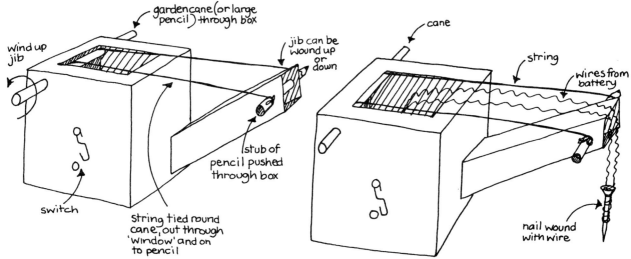

garden cane (or large pencil) through box

wind up jib

jib can be wound up or down

stub of pencil pushed through box

switch

string tied round cane, out through 'window' and on to pencil

cane

string

wires from battery

nail wound with wire

You may already have a toy crane that is large enough to carry your electro-magnet. If not you can make one quite easily with cardboard boxes. Find a box that is cube shaped and about 20 cm (8 in) long. You will also need a

long thin box or card tube about 30 cm (12 in) long, some string, a pencil and a thin garden cane about 30 cm (12 in) long.

Cut a 'window' out of the top of the box so that you can drop the battery and wires of your electro-magnet inside. Fix a simple switch where you can turn it on and off easily somewhere on the side of the box. Make a hole at the bottom of the front face of the box and push the end of the tube into it so that it juts out like the jib of a crane.

Make two small holes either side about 2 cm (1 in) from the end of the tube and push the pencil through. Make another two holes in the sides of the box towards the top, rear corners and push the garden cane through. Tie a length of string or strong thread to each end of the pencil and tie the other ends round the cane, passing the string through the top 'window' of the box. By winding the cane the strings can be made to raise or lower the jib. Finally, hang the iron nail and wire coil from the end of your crane's jib and connect it to the battery and switch.

To use your crane simply switch on the power and lower the jib to bring the nail down onto a pile of pins or paper clips. Wind up the string to raise the jib and lift the pins clear. Swing your crane to the side, switch off the power and drop the pins where you need them.

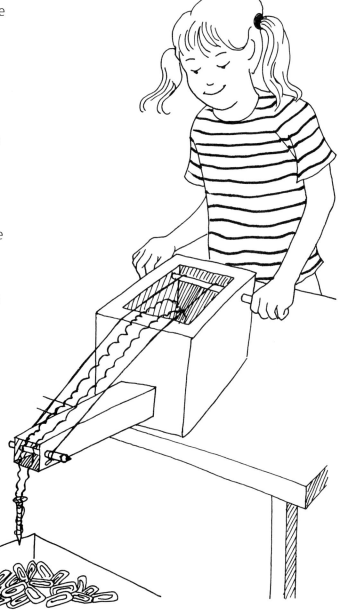

lectricity

Electricity is one of the most important forms of power that we use today. Look around your own home and notice how many things need electricity to work. In the kitchen you might find a washing machine and drier, dishwasher, and hob, extractor fan, microwave oven, fridge and freezer, kettle, oven, food mixer and processor, as well as a vacuum cleaner and iron.

Think of the ways in which we can communicate today: we can receive news and entertainment through the television and radio; we can call almost anywhere in the world by telephone; we can watch films using a video recorder and listen to music on records, tapes or CD discs. Even a simple thing like turning on the light we take for granted, yet most of these technological marvels are very new. Ask your Grandparents how many of these things they had when they were young, you will be surprised how few.

Getting started

The enormous speed of technological invention and improvement owes a great deal to electrical power. You can use this power for yourself by buying a few simple items from any good electrical shop. You will need two or three small torch bulbs. Ask for ones that take between 3 to 6 volts of electricity to make them light up. Ask for some cheap bulb holders too, and a small screwdriver to undo the screws on the holders. You will also need a 4.5 volt bicycle lamp battery.

Lastly you will need some lengths of wire with about 2 cm of the plastic insulation stripped from each end. (This can be done with wire strippers or a pair of scissors, but you may need to ask an adult to help you).

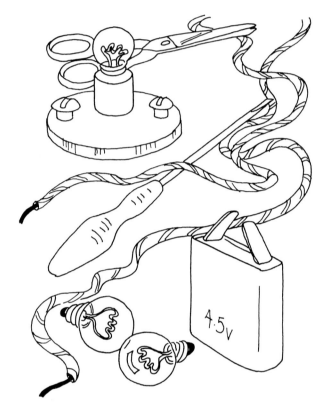

REMEMBER, ALTHOUGH IT IS QUITE SAFE TO EXPERIMENT WITH BATTERIES AND BULBS, NEVER PLAY WITH THE MAINS ELECTRICITY, IT COULD KILL YOU.

A simple circuit

You will need the battery, two paper clips, two wires, a bulb and a bulb holder. Use a small screwdriver to attach the wires to the bulb holder. Wind the other end of each wire around a paper clip. Electricity needs to flow from one terminal of a battery through the bulb and back to the other terminal of the battery to make a

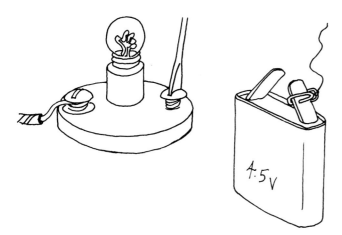

battery terminal through the first bulb then on to the second bulb and back to the other battery terminal. You will find that the bulbs appear quite dim and, when you unscrew one of the bulbs, they both go out.

The second circuit is called a 'parallel' circuit. Each bulb is connected to the battery with its own wires and has its own circuit. The two bulbs shine almost as brightly as one and if you unscrew one of the bulbs, the other bulb stays alight. The picture also shows a second way of making a parallel circuit.

complete ring or circuit. Push one of the clips onto a battery terminal and touch the other paper clip onto the second terminal. The bulb will flash on. Does it matter which way round you touch the battery terminals with your wires?

Two bulbs from one battery

For this investigation you will need two bulbs in holders, some wires and the 4.5 volt battery.

There are two different circuits you can make with your bulbs. Try the first, it is called a 'series' circuit. The electricity flows out of one

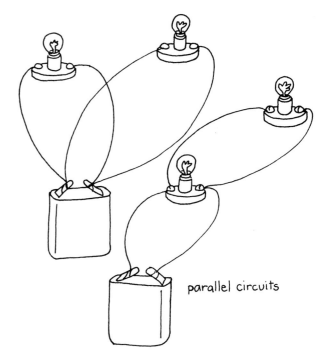

parallel circuits

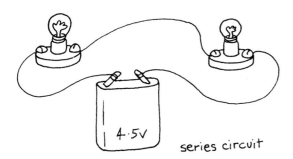

series circuit

If you make a model that needs two lights or perhaps a light and a motor or a buzzer, you can use the parallel circuit to make them all work just from one battery.

Switching on and off

It can be very useful to be able to switch a bulb on and off when you like without having to unscrew wires. You will need a small off-cut of wood about 10 cm by 7 cm (4 in by 3 in), two drawing pins and a paper clip as well as your battery, bulb and holder and some wires.

Set up the circuit as shown. Push the drawing pins into the wood about 5 cm (2 in) apart. Wind a wire from the battery around one of the pins and push it firmly into the wood, then trap a wire to the bulb holder and a paper clip under the second drawing pin.

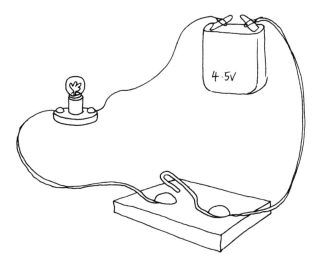

4.5V

When you push the paper clip across to touch the other drawing pin, the paper clip, which is made from metal, conducts the electricity across the gap between the pins and completes the circuit, making the bulb light up. To turn it off again, simply move the paper clip away.

Upstairs downstairs

Use a simple switch to turn lights on and off on models that you have made. You could build a doll's house from a large cardboard box and put lights in the rooms with paper clip switches.

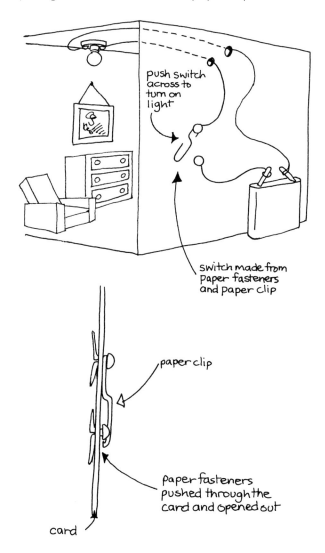

push switch across to turn on light

switch made from paper fasteners and paper clip

paper clip

paper fasteners pushed through the card and opened out

card

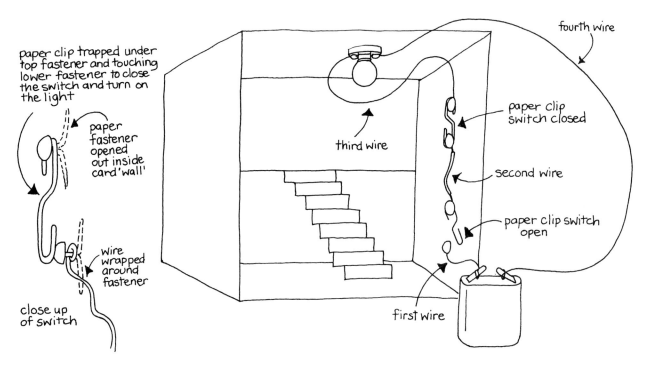

paper clip trapped under top fastener and touching lower fastener to close the switch and turn on the light

paper fastener opened out inside card 'wall'

wire wrapped around fastener

close up of switch

third wire

fourth wire

paper clip switch closed

second wire

paper clip switch open

first wire

Make stairs by folding a long strip of card into a concertina shape and glue them in place. Can you think of a way to turn on a light that is upstairs with a switch that is downstairs and turn it off again from upstairs, like the lights for the stairs in a real home? You don't need two batteries or even two sets of wires. Run a wire from one battery terminal to a switch. Take another wire from the first switch to the second switch and join the bulb to the second switch with a wire. Finally join the bulb to the second battery terminal.

Close the upstairs switch, but leave the downstairs switch open. If you want to put the light on upstairs you now close the lower switch and the bulb will light. Once upstairs you can open the upper switch and it will go off again.

Build a lighthouse

You can make a light house from a cardboard tube or an empty washing up liquid bottle. Ask an adult to help you pull the squeezy jet out of the end and to cut the bottom of the bottle off with scissors. (If you push the point of the scissors through the plastic it is then easy to cut round.)

Connect two wires about 40 cm (16 in) long to the screw terminals of a bulb holder, then push the bulb holder up into the top of the bottle so that the bulb sticks out of the top. Connect one of the wires to your battery and the other to your simple switch so that when the paper clip is moved to touch the drawing pin the light comes on.

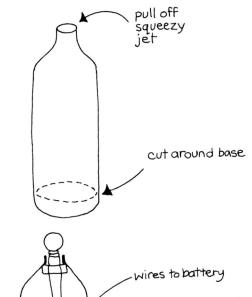

pull off
squeezy
jet

cut around base

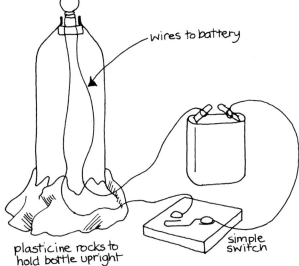

Wires to battery

plasticine rocks to
hold bottle upright

simple
switch

Sending messages

Another useful switch is called a 'push to make' switch. This is made in exactly the same way as the first one, except that the paper clip is bent up at an angle so that it is positioned above the second drawing pin. To turn on the light you have to push down on the paper clip, when you let go it springs back up again and the light goes out.

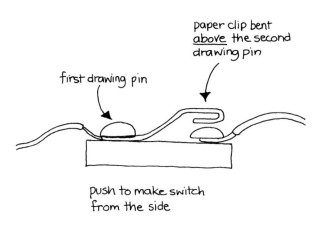

paper clip bent
<u>above</u> the second
drawing pin

first drawing pin

push to make switch
from the side

Stand the tube or bottle on plasticine 'rocks' and cover the bottle or tube with paper that you have painted to look like a lighthouse. You may also be lucky enough to be able to buy a special flashing bulb from an electrical shop which will make your model even more realistic.

This kind of switch can be used to make a morse code key. If you make two of them and get some long lengths of wire (bell wire is perfect) you can send messages to a friend in another room. Set up the circuit as shown. When you press on your morse key your light will flash on and off, so you can see the message that you are sending, and the light in the next room will flash at the same time. Your friend can reply by pushing on her switch.

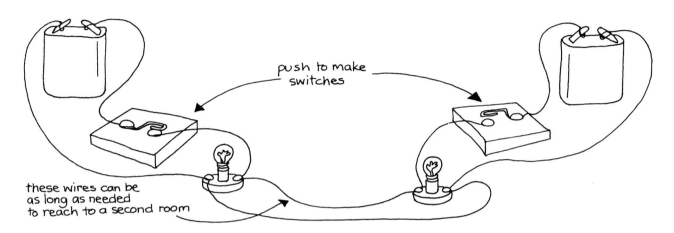

push to make switches

these wires can be as long as needed to reach to a second room

See if you can make up your own code or find out about the morse code at your local library.

Traffic lights

The three coloured lights in traffic lights turn on and off in the same set pattern. A green light is always followed by amber then red, but, before shining green again, the red and amber lights come on together.

To make a model of some traffic lights you will need three bulbs and holders, some wires and a battery, as well as a piece of wood, drawing pins and a paper clip for the switch. To turn three lights on and off to show a green light, amber and then red is quite easy, the difficulty comes in getting the red and amber to shine together before switching to the green.

Screw, tape or tie the three bulb holders to a stick of wood and stand it upright in some plasticene or nail or glue a small square of wood or thick card to the bottom so that the stick will stand upright and look like traffic lights. To make the effect even better, paint or

colour the bulbs with felt tipped pens or wrap red, yellow and green cellophane around the bulbs. Some sweets are wrapped in coloured see-through cellophane which may be just the colours you're looking for.

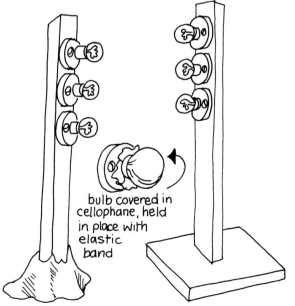

bulb covered in cellophane, held in place with elastic band

Wiring up

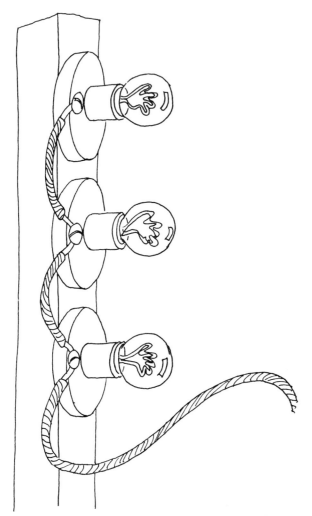

Connect a piece of wire about 40 cm (16 in) long between one of the battery terminals and one of the screws on the green light's bulb holder. Also join the green light's screw to one on the amber light and the red light with short pieces of wire.

Get a small block of wood like the ones used to make simple switches, four drawing pins, a paper clip and four pieces of wire about 30 cm (12 in) long. Push the four drawing pins into the wood block as shown, with three on one side and one on the other. Notice that the top two are close together, this is very important.

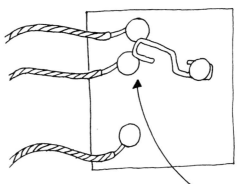

when paper clip touches top two drawing pins the red and yellow lights shine together

Now join the second screw terminal of the red light to the top drawing pin with one of the wires. Do the same with the amber light, connecting it with the middle pin and then join the green light to the bottom drawing pin. Finally use the fourth wire to connect the second battery terminal to the single drawing pin on the right of the block, remember also to trap the paper clip under the pin to act as a switch.

To make your traffic lights work turn the paper clip to touch the bottom pin and the green light will shine. Move the paper clip to the middle pin and the amber light comes on,

then move the clip to the top pin and the red light will shine. To make the red and amber lights come to together simply position the paper clip so the it touches both top and middle drawing pins at the same time (that is why they were placed close together).

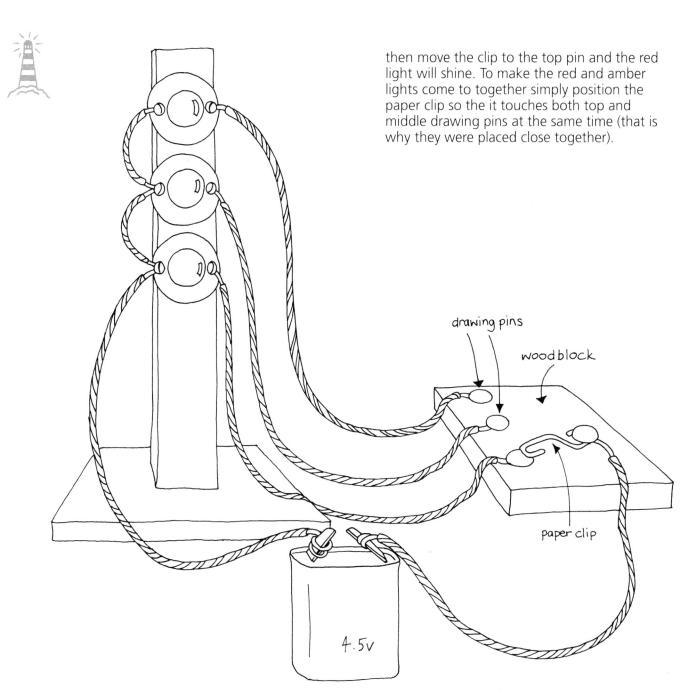

drawing pins

wood block

paper clip

4.5v

A pressure switch alarm

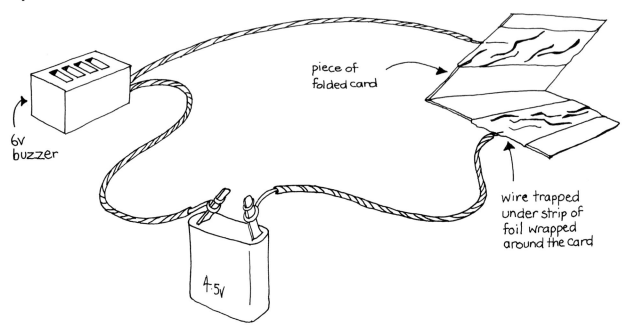

piece of folded card

6v buzzer

4.5v

wire trapped under strip of foil wrapped around the card

Another interesting type of switch is a pressure switch. This works when something or someone treads or pushes down on the switch, setting off a light or buzzer.

It can be made very easily with a thin piece of card about 15 cms (6 in) long by 8 cm (3 in) wide, some cooking foil and a little paste or tape.

Make a simple circuit with a light bulb or buzzer like the one shown with the paper clip switch but, instead of trapping the wires under drawing pins pressed into a piece of wood, leave the ends of the wires free. Fold the piece of card in half and wrap strips of foil round the top and bottom flap. Make sure that you trap one of the ends of the two spare wires under each strip of foil.

The gap between the two strips of foil stops the circuit from being complete but, as soon as someone pushes down on the top flap of the card, the two strips of foil will touch and the bulb or buzzer will come on. For extra fun, position the switch near to a doorway so that any unsuspecting person walking in will tread on the switch and set off your alarm.

The wibbly wobbly way

This game is great fun, and so easy to make. All you need is a wire coat hanger, a pair of strong pliers, a block of wood about 40cm (16in) long and 15cm (6in) wide, some wire staples and a hammer, as well as a battery and two wires

about 40 cm (16in) long, a bulb and a short wire.

Use the short wire to join one of the screw terminals of the bulb holder to one of the battery terminals.

Ask an adult to help you unbend the coat hanger and cut a piece about 20cm (8in) long from one end using the pliers. Make a loop at the end of the piece of coat hanger and wind the bared end of one of the wires around the other end, holding it in place with some Sellotape. Connect the other end of the wire to the second screw terminal in the bulb holder.

Bend the rest of the coat hanger into an interesting wibbly wobbly shape and staple its ends firmly to the block of wood. Make sure that one end of your second wire is also trapped under one of the wire staples. Connect the other end of the wire to the second battery terminal. Wrap Sellotape around the ends of the wobbly wire, these will be the start and finish points.

To play the game make sure the circuit is set up correctly then hook the loop over the wobbly wire and try to move it along the wire to the other end without touching it. If you touch the wire the light will flash and you will have to start again. Try it on your friends and see who has the steadiest hand.

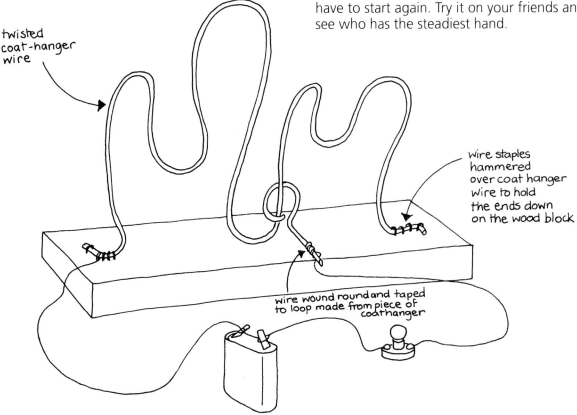

twisted coat-hanger wire

wire staples hammered over coat hanger wire to hold the ends down on the wood block

wire wound round and taped to loop made from piece of coathanger

The mystery question game

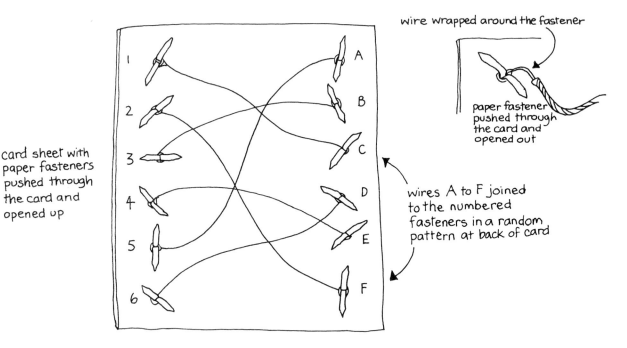

wire wrapped around the fastener

paper fastener
pushed through
the card and
opened out

card sheet with
paper fasteners
pushed through
the card and
opened up

wires A to F joined
to the numbered
fasteners in a random
pattern at back of card

This is a really exciting game to make because only the right answers will flash the light.

You will need a sheet of thick card about 30 to 40 cm. (12 to 16 in) square, 12 brass paper fasteners, (the kind that you can push through paper or card and open out at the back to hold them in place), some wires, a battery, a bulb and holder.

The question and answer board is set up by pushing the paper fasteners through the card in two columns of six, evenly spaced out down the sides. The point of a pair of scissors can be used to make small holes in the card to make it easier to push the fasteners through.

The secret of the game is in the way the fasteners are joined together by wires at the back of the board. Turn the board over and wind the bare end of a wire around each fastener down the right hand side of the board. Then each wire is joined to the paper fasteners on the left hand side, but in a mixed up way so that no fastener on the right is joined to its immediate neighbour on the left.

Turn the board over to the front again and write six questions, one next to each of the paper fasteners down the left hand side. Join one of the battery terminals to a screw terminal on the bulb holder with a shorter length of wire. Connect a wire to the second battery terminal and another wire to the second screw terminal on the bulb holder. Wind the other ends of each wire around a paper clip.

Playing the game

Hold one of the paper clips against the stud of the paper fastener that is next to question 1 on the left hand side of the board. Touch the other clip to each of the fastener studs on the right side. The light will flash on when you touch the one that is connected by a wire at the back to the left-hand fastener. Write the answer to question 1 here. Repeat this for each of the questions.

To play the game ask a friend to read a question and guess the answer. Show her how to hold a paper clip against the question stud and then touch the other paper clip on the stud next to her chosen answer, the light will flash on only when she chooses the right answer.

You can change the questions as often as you like and, if your friends get to know the question-answer pattern, you can change the wiring at the back of the board as well.

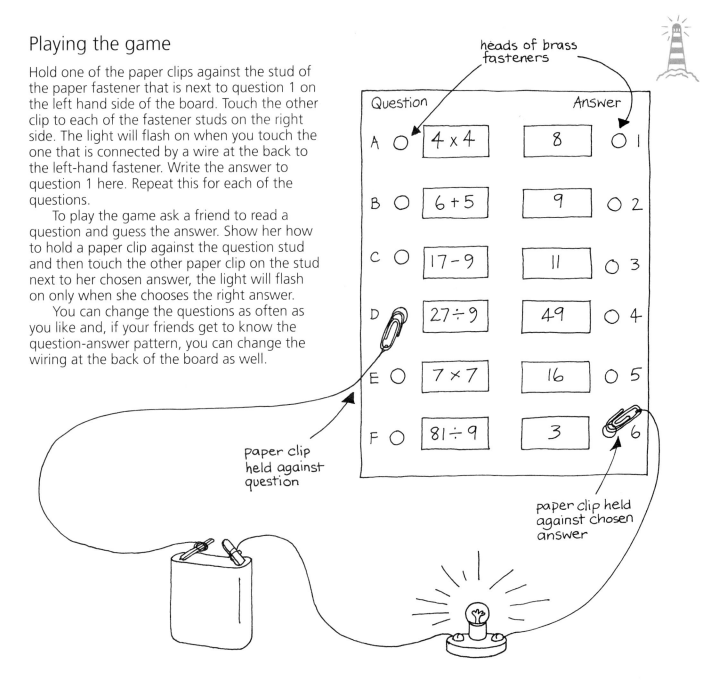

heads of brass fasteners

Question   Answer

A 4×4 8   1

B $6 + 5$ 9   2

C $17 - 9$ 11   3

D $27 \div 9$ 49   4

E 7×7 16   5

F $81 \div 9$ 3   6

paper clip held against question

paper clip held against chosen answer

Cogs, gears and tubes

The development of the bicycle

The earliest kind of bicycle was called a 'hobby horse'. It had a frame made of wood and iron wheels. The rider sat astride the frame and pushed it along with his feet, free-wheeling down hills. With no brakes and primitive steering it must have been a difficult and dangerous contraption to ride.

The idea of fitting pedals to the front wheel made riding easier and solid rubber tyres gave a bit more comfort over bumpy, cobbled roads. It was discovered that, by making the front wheel larger, one turn of the pedals would make the bicycle go much further and so it could be ridden faster. This was how the 'penny farthing' came to be made with its enormous front wheel and tiny back wheel. Penny farthings were certainly fast, but to mount them and cycle safely must have been very difficult.

Three things helped to change these early machines into the bicycle we know today. The first was the use of hollow steel tubes, welded together in triangular patterns to make strong, but light frames. The second was the invention of pneumatic tyres by John Boyd Dunlop, a Scottish veterinary surgeon. He began experiments with air-filled tyres to cushion his son's bicycle against the bumpy cobbles after the family doctor had prescribed cycling to improve the boy's health. The third development was the use of toothed cogs fitted to the pedals and the rear wheel, joined by a continuous chain.

Cogs and gears

If you are lucky enough to own a bicycle you can do some interesting investigations on it.

Turn your bike upside down so that it rests on the handle bars and saddle. Carefully count the number of teeth on the large front cog. You may need to mark one of them with a felt-tipped pen to remember where you started counting. Now count the number on the back cog. If you have more than one gear, count the teeth on the gear that the chain is around. Now you can show your mathematical skill by dividing the number from the larger cog by the number from the smaller cog; you may need a calculator to help you. For example there might be 81 teeth on the first and 45 on the second. If you divide 81 by 45 you get 1.8. This is called the gear ratio, but what does it mean?

Ask a friend to help you to do some counting. With the bike still upside down, set the pedals vertically so that they are exactly straight up and down. Mark the very top point of the rear tyre with some chalk. Now turn the pedals slowly exactly ten full turns while your friend counts the number of times the rear wheel goes round. Now divide the number of times the wheel turned by 10 (the number of turns of the pedals) and this will be the number of times that the rear wheel turns for one turn of the pedals. For example, if the rear wheel turned 14 times, one turn of the pedals would make the wheel turn 1.4 times.

If it was 21 times, one turn would make the rear wheel turn 2.1 times or just over twice. The important thing to notice is how close the number is to the gear ratio that you have already calculated.

If your bike has lots of gears you can work out their ratios and you will discover that the rear wheel will turn the exact number of times shown by the gear ratio. So, a ratio of 2.7 will mean that the rear wheel will turn 27 times with 10 full turns of the pedals.

Gears to go faster

If you try the investigation on gears you will also discover that the greater the difference in size between the front and rear cogs, the bigger the gear ratio and the greater the number of times the rear wheel goes round for each turn of the pedals. This was how bicycle manufacturers were able to make their machines go fast without the need for an enormous front wheel.

With a large front cog and a tiny rear one, the back wheel can be made to turn as much as three times for just one turn of the pedals, which would take the bike three times further than if the pedals were joined directly to the wheel. There is only one problem that all bike riders soon discover; the smaller the rear cog, the harder it is to turn the pedals.

Try it for yourself. If you or a friend has a bike with lots of gears, turn it upside down as before. With the largest cog on the rear wheel selected, turn the pedals slowly. Feel how little effort is needed to turn the pedals. Now change gear to the smallest cog and try turning the pedals once more. Although the wheel turns faster, the effort you need to turn the pedals is much greater.

This is why racing cycles have lots of gears; larger ones for riding up hills, (the bike goes more slowly, but the pedals are easier to turn) and very small rear gears for travelling fast down hill or on flat roads. The latest mountain bikes can have as many as 18 gear ratios, some made especially for cycling slowly but easily up very steep slopes.

Changing direction

Cogs and gears are not only used for changing the speed of moving parts of a machines, many cogs are used to change the direction of movement as well. Cogs have been used in this way for hundreds of years. If you are able to visit a working windmill or watermill you will find inside that there are some enormous cogs. They are often made from oak or apple wood and the 'crown' wheel of a windmill changes the direction of the turning sails at the side of the mill so that a long wooden shaft, running down the centre of the mill, can be turned round and round. This shaft is connected by other cogs to the sets of mill stones that grind the wheat.

Make your own cogs

To make cogs accurately enough to change speed is very difficult, but it is much easier to make cogs to change direction. All you need are two cotton reels, 16 used matches and some glue. Cut the matches with a craft knife so that they are all 2 cm (just under 1 inch) long. Glue them onto the cotton reels, 8 on each, so that they jut out from the edge as shown. Leave the hole through the cotton reel clear. When the glue has hardened and the matches are firmly set, push pencils through the holes in the cotton reels so that they are free to turn.

Hold one of your cogs at right angles to the other so that the match stick 'teeth' mesh together. Now, if you turn one of them, the other will also turn. Notice that they turn in opposite directions and the movement of one is at right angles to the other. Cogs that change direction in this way are used in the rear axles of many cars. The rotation of the engine is turned through 90 degrees by cogs in what is called the differential gear so that the wheels can turn to drive the car along.

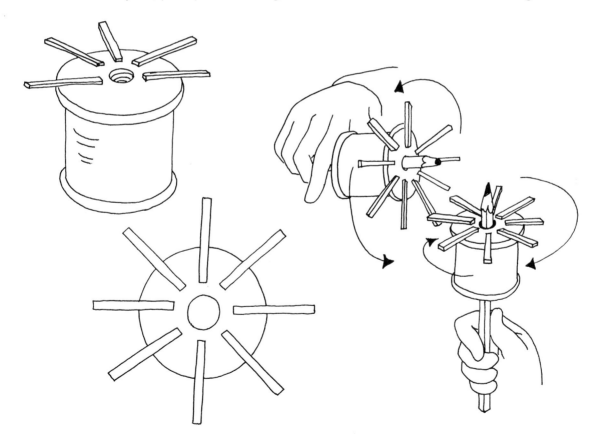

The strength of tubes

Tubes, such as those used in bicycle frames, can be light but strong. The shape is very important. Even something as weak as a sheet of newspaper can be made much stronger by changing its shape. Try this investigation. Take a sheet of newspaper and lay it between two chair seats. It is so thin and flimsy that it can barely stop from folding and falling to the floor.

It certainly could not support very much weight.

Now roll the sheet into a tight tube and lay the tube across the gap. The tube shape is much stronger and the sheet can bridge the gap easily. Hang a yogurt pot from the centre of the tube with some thin string or cotton. Load the pot gently with marbles or small stones. How many can the tube support before it finally folds and falls to the floor?

Bridge building

A single tube would not make a very successful
bridge, it would be very difficult to walk or
drive across, but several tubes, side by side
could make a firm base for a bridge. Roll 5 or 6
tight tubes from sheets of newspaper, you can
hold them in shape with pieces of sticky tape.
Lay them across the gap between two chairs
and place a piece of paper or thin card on top
of the tubes to form a road way. How many toy
cars, stones or marbles can you lay on your
bridge before it begins to collapse? You will be
surprised how strong it can be. As an
experiment, some engineers built a bridge
entirely from cardboard that was strong enough
to support the weight of a lorry!

More strength tests

Tubes can be strong in other ways. Bridges need to be supported. One way to do this is to rest the roadway on piles driven into the ground or river bed. This can be done by sinking a large steel tube in place and filling it with concrete. The pile is very strong and it will support a lot of weight. Try it for yourself, all you need are 10 pieces of card about the size and thickness of a post card and sticky tape.

Roll one of the cards into a tube about 8 cm (3 in) high and 3 cm (1 in) across. Hold it in place with a piece of sticky tape. Stand the tube on its end on a hard, flat surface and balance a book on top. Now slowly and carefully load more books, one at a time, on top. If you run out of books try anything heavy but be sure to balance them well. How much weight can the tube support before it collapses?

You can amaze your friends and family by rolling the other pieces of card into similar tube shapes. Hold the tubes in shape with sticky tape just as before. Place the tubes on a hard, flat floor in three rows of three about 10 cm (4 in) apart. Place a tray or flat board on top of the tubes and ask for a small volunteer. (Choose the smallest, lightest child). Ask someone to help you support your volunteer's arms while he or she gently stands on the centre of the tray. You must be very careful not to disturb the tubes, they must stay perfectly upright.

When she is in place and well balanced slowly release her arms until she is standing alone on the tray held up by only 9 post cards. This trick is amazing to watch and with a few more tubes and a lot of care, even a large adult can be supported.

Tube towers

Tubes can be used to make strong shapes. Have you ever seen scaffolding that is placed around the site of a new building so that the builders can climb over it to reach all parts of the structure? Towers and masts can be built from tubes reaching hundreds of feet in the air.

Collect as many large, plastic drinking straws as you can and attempt to build the tallest tower possible. Think of the shape of electricity pylons; a large, square base and triangular criss-cross patterns of girders rising to the top. You can join the straws together by pushing one inside another, or you can use sticky tape or dressmakers pins (but mind your fingers). Furry pipe cleaners make excellent joining pieces and you can twist them together to make three and four-way joints.

Try this challenge, build a tower that not only goes upwards, but outwards too. Can you make something that looks like one of those tall cranes used on building sites that is strong enough to support the weight of small toy at the end?

pieces of pipe cleaner wound together to make 3 and 4-way joints

straws pushed onto pipe cleaner joint

Energy and forces

Saving energy

The world is becoming more and more energy conscious. Every building in developed countries uses energy to heat and light it. Machines and vehicles consume vast amounts of energy to make them work. Energy is supplied as gas or electricity, or it might be in the form of fuel such as petrol, coal or oil. The more the world develops industries the greater are the demands on energy supply.

The problem that faces us is the fact that most of our energy for heat, light and power is made from fossil fuels. These are things like coal and oil that have been formed by heat and pressure deep under the ground over millions of years. Although we are using up our reserves of fossil fuels at a faster and faster rate, they are not being replaced. There may come a time in the not too distant future when our fuel reserves finally run out. Too much energy is wasted unnecessarily. That is why scientists, engineers and governments are beginning to do more to save energy.

One simple example is the home you live in. How many lights get left on in rooms that are unoccupied? How much heat is lost during the winter through doors and windows left open? Many homes are now insulated to stop heat being lost, but what does 'insulation' mean?

The teapot test

One way to do this investigation is to get 10 identical teapots! However, it isn't very likely that, even in the biggest tea drinking family, you will find that many teapots. Don't worry, you can do the experiment just as easily with empty tins or drinks cans.

You will also need some insulating materials such as the following items; a large newspaper, a woolly scarf or jumper, tin foil, plastic wrap or bags, cardboard, polystyrene tiles or packing, a box large enough for a tin to stand in that can be filled with grass cuttings or sawdust, a similar empty box, a pair of large cotton socks and woollen ones, old nylon tights and pieces of material such as net curtaining, fur fabric and any other fabrics that you may be able to get. Finally, it isn't essential to have a thermometer, but your results will be far more accurate if you can use one.

Insulating the cans

To set up the investigation all you need to do is to wrap each tin in a different fabric or material. If necessary, hold the things in place with some sticky tape or string. Try one tin covered in a thin cotton sock and another in a thick woolly sock. The can inside the box can be surrounded by soil, sand, grass cuttings or sawdust and the result can be compared with a can left in an empty box. Leave one can completely uncovered, this will be your control to compare the others against.

The cans need to be filled with water that is at the same temperature. Do NOT use boiling water. The easiest way is to run the hot tap and use a jug to pour the same amount of hot water into each tin. If you have a thermometer, take the temperature of the water and make a note of the time.

After exactly 30 minutes take the temperature of the water in each tin. Do you expect them to be the same? Which tin do you

expect to be the warmest and which will hold the coldest water?

If you have not got a thermometer pour a little water over the back of your hand and compare this with the water from another can. Put the cans in order from the one that you feel is the warmest to the one that is the coldest. You can ask a friend to help with your comparisons to see if you agree.

When a can has hot water poured into it, the heat is conducted through the metal and is lost to the air. If the heat can be trapped by putting a layer of something around the tin the heat will be lost more slowly. This is called insulating the can. What makes the best insulator? Are cotton socks better than woollen ones? Is an empty box better than cling film? If you had to keep something, or someone, as warm as possible what would you wrap them in?

Giving friction the slip

Another way to save energy is to make parts of engines and machines move as freely as possible. Wherever one part of a machine rubs against another, heat is produced and the parts begin to wear. This is called friction. You can feel the effect of friction just by rubbing your hands together hard, they soon feel very warm. Slide from top to bottom down a rope and you could get friction burns on your hands. If you can reduce friction and things can slide more easily they will not get so hot or wear so quickly.

Make your hands soapy and now rub them together. Instead of getting warm they just slide over one another. Oil and grease can do the same for engine parts. The oil 'lubricates' the moving parts making them slippery and reducing the friction.

Ball bearings

Another way in which parts of machines can be made to move more easily is to use a bearing. Where a shaft runs through a hole, such as an axle through the hub of a wheel, the wheel can turn more easily if the hole is lined with steel balls. This is called a ball bearing.

You can see the effect of using ball bearings in a very simple way. Find a tin that has a deep rim around the outside, such as a syrup tin. Remove the lid and lay a large, heavy book on the top. Try to spin the book around, it hardly moves at all. Now place marbles all round the rim of the tin and replace the book. When you try to spin the book now it moves very easily, rolling on the marbles.

Think of the wheels of a skate board or roller skates. The wheels are fixed to the ends

of axles. The are made to spin as freely as possible by reducing the friction with ball bearings and a little oil. This allows the skates to roll quickly and easily. But there is another problem, if the skate wheels could not grip the pavement surface the skater would slip and slide all over the place and get nowhere. If the soles of our shoes or the tyres of cars did not grip the road we would continually fall over and cars would spin wildly out of control. Sometimes increasing friction can be very important to help to improve grip.

Getting to grips with friction

Remember how slippery your hands were when covered in soap? Try to open a bottle cap or turn a door knob with soapy hands, it is almost impossible. Only when you have rinsed off the soap and dried your hands can you get a grip. Water can make things slippery and frozen water, ice, is very slippery. That is why pedestrians and drivers have to be so careful in wet or icy conditions.

What kinds of things have good grip and which slide more easily? Collect a number of objects such as a stone, a small block of wood, a rubber, a matchbox, an ice cube and a coin. You will also need a large, flat sheet of wood, card or plastic such as a board or tray.

Place the objects side by side along one end of the board and slowly and gently raise it up. Watch carefully to see which object begins to slide first. Can you guess which it will be and which is last to move, which has the greatest friction?

Does the weight of the object matter? Will the matchbox slide sooner if it is filled with heavy coins? You can also try a small cardboard box on your slope. At what angle does it begin to move? Now try again after placing a bag of flour inside the box. What angle does the box now tilt to before moving?

Large and heavy loads are very difficult to drag across the ground because of friction.

Consider the difficulties faced by the builders of structures such as Stonehenge or the great pyramids of Egypt. How were the enormous slabs of stone moved? Historians believe that they may have used tree trunks as rollers. Try this for yourself by trying to drag a shoe box full of stones across the floor. Now lay a number of round pencils on the ground and lay the box on them. When the box is pulled, the pencils roll and the box slides across them much more easily. As the box moves, pencils can be taken from the back and replaced at the front, just as the pyramid builders would have done with their tree trunks.

Four wheels on my wagon

If a slice is cut from the trunk of a tree it will roll easily. The Sumarians were the first to discover how to join a round shaped piece of wood to an axle in such a way that it could turn freely.

This was a tremendous technological breakthrough because, instead of having to continually fetch and carry large tree trunk rollers, the axles could be attached to the underside of a box-shaped container that would roll along on its own wheels. This was how the first carts were made and, when horses or oxen were harnessed to the wagons, large loads could be moved quite easily.

You can make your own wheeled cart very easily. Find a cardboard box that is about 20 to 25 cm (8 to 10 in) long and 10 cm (4 in) wide. About the size of an ordinary house brick. Attach an elastic band to the front of the box and place some weights such as conkers, marbles or stones inside. Put the box on a flat, smooth surface and pull gently on the elastic band to take up the slack. Measure the length of the elastic band. Now pull on the band until the box just begins to move. How long is the band now? It takes quite considerable effort to make the box move.

Adding wheels

To put wheels on your box, you will need two axles. These can be made from any thin, rounded sticks such as dowel rod, garden cane or even rounded pencils or knitting needles would do. Join the axles to the box with elastic bands as shown.

For the wheels you can use cotton reels, if the axles are long enough, or else round cheese slice boxes with a hole punched through the centre with the point of some scissors make excellent cart wheels. You may even have wooden or plastic wheels in your toy box that you could use, or you can cut circles from a piece of thick card. Whatever you choose, push your wheels onto the ends of the axles and be sure that they turn quite freely. Stop them from falling off the axles by putting a blob of plasticene or a few turns of sticky tape on the ends.

Now put your model back on the floor and pull on the elastic band once more. Do you have to pull as hard to make your cart move? How long is the elastic band, is it shorter or longer than before?

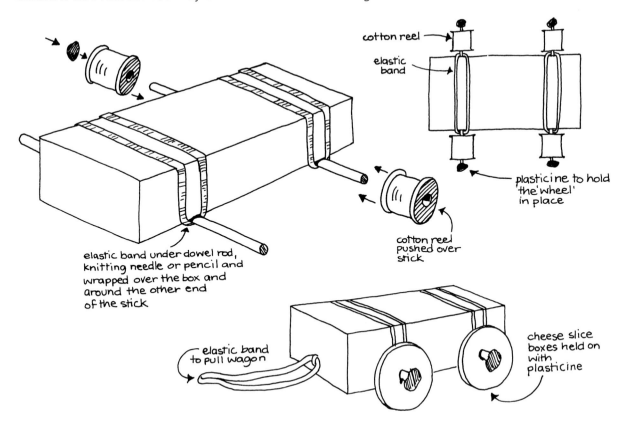

cotton reel

elastic band

plasticine to hold the 'wheel' in place

elastic band under dowel rod, knitting needle or pencil and wrapped over the box and around the other end of the stick

cotton reel pushed over stick

elastic band to pull wagon

cheese slice boxes held on with plasticine

Improving the design

There is no one way of building a cart, or car or lorry or any other form of transport. The design of a vehicle, that means its shape and how it is made, can affect the way that it moves. The shape of cars and lorries has changed enormously over the last 50 years as designers learn more and more about reducing weight and drag as well as improving performance and saving fuel.

If you are able to make two wheeled carts, you can try an interesting investigation with them. Perhaps one of your carts has small, wide wheels, such as cotton reels. The other may have large, narrow wheels. Which one will travel the greatest distance with a single push?

To test your carts more fairly you will need to use a flat board of card or wood as a slope. Prop one end up on some books and place one of your carts at the top of the slope. Don't push, just let it run down the slope and across the floor. How far does it travel from the bottom of the slope? Now try with your other cart, which one goes the furthest?

It may be fairer to repeat your test a few times to see if there is one cart that always goes further than the other. If one of the carts is always left far behind, look at the design of the cart. Look especially at its wheels and how freely they turn on their axles. See if you can improve its performance by changing the size of the wheels or by making them spin more easily.

Wearing well

The effects of friction can be very costly. Think of the wear that the seat of a skirt or pair of trousers gets during a busy day, constantly being rubbed by whatever we sit on. Some fabrics can be very hard wearing, but others look shabby and worn very quickly. Here is one way of testing fabric samples to discover their wear resistance.

You will need oddments of material about 30 cm (12 in) square, a block of wood about 20 cm (8 in) square which will be the base block, sheets of medium grade glass paper and a rubbing block (a block of wood about 15 cm (6 in) long and 5 cm (2 in) wide.

Stretch a square of fabric over the base block and use drawing pins, pushed in around the sides, to hold it firmly in place. Cut a strip of glass paper, 15 cm (6 in) wide and wrap it tightly around the rubbing block. Secure the glass paper with a couple of drawing pins.

Now rub the glass paper over the centre of the fabric with firm, steady stokes until you have given it exactly 100 rubs. Unpin the square of fabric and examine it carefully. Hold it up to a window so that the light can shine through it. Compare the central, rubbed area with the untouched outer edge. How much wear can you detect? Some fabric samples may actually have worn right through.

To make this test as fair as possible try to rub with the same amount of pressure and speed each time. Use a fresh strip of glass paper for each test and use the test to compare similar materials. For example, use squares cut from old denims to find the strongest wearing denim material. Try it with squares taken from old school skirts or trousers. Who knows, you may even be able to recommend the best buys for the greatest wear resistance.

The magic wobbly tin

This is a great trick that is so simple to make. Find an empty tin that has a removable lid, such as a cocoa or drinking chocolate tin. Ask an adult to help you make two holes in the lid and two holes in the base with a large nail and a hammer. Make the holes evenly spaced either side of the centre about 1 cm (a quarter of an inch) in from the rim. Get a large, heavy steel nut and a long elastic band.

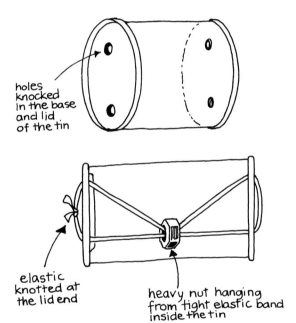

holes knocked in the base and lid of the tin

elastic knotted at the lid end

heavy nut hanging from tight elastic band inside the tin

To set up the wobbly tin, cut the elastic band so that you have a long strip of elastic. Thread the ends through the two holes in the base of the tin and pass the ends through the metal nut. Finally push the ends of the elastic through the holes in the lid, push the lid firmly onto the tin and tie the ends of the elastic

together so that it is quite tight but still loose enough to be twisted or pulled easily. The band should be tight enough to stop the nut from scraping or banging against the side of the tin.

Roll the tin gently across a smooth floor and watch. The tin soon wobbles to a halt, then miraculously begins to roll back towards you, ending up by rolling backwards and forwards until it shudders to a halt. What is happening inside the tin is that the heavy nut does not roll with the tin, but, as it is resting on the elastic band it winds up the band. When the can stops rolling, the elastic begins to unwind, pulling the can back the other way.

What's in the tin?

Let us suppose that you have two tins and both their labels have come off. You know that one of the tins contains dog food and the other contains fruit salad. Both tins weight about the same and look the same, how can you tell which is which without opening them?

This seems an impossible task, but the answer is remarkably simple. Rest a sheet of thick card or a thin, wooden board on a book to make a shallow slope. Place the tins side by side at the top of the slope and let go. The tin that rolls the furthest across the floor is the one that contains the dog food!

Try the test again to make sure, but on each occasion one tin will roll further than the other.

Why does this happen? It is all to do with the contests of the tin. With the wobbly tin

experiment the nut does not turn with the tin. This also happens with tins that contain sloppy things like pieces of fruit in lots of watery syrup. When the tin rolls down the slope the fruit takes time to begin to move inside the tin. This is called inertia, (say in-er-sha). This creates a lot of drag that holds the tin back and stops it from rolling easily.

The dog food on the other hand is usually quite solid inside the tin so that it rolls with the tin without drag and the tin rolls much further than the tin of fruit.

You can even do a survey of tins of baked beans this way. Which tin has the most beans? By rolling the tins as before it will be the tin that rolls the furthest that is the most tightly packed. Those tins that contain lots of tomato sauce will have sloppy contents that will cause drag and hold the tin back.

Elastic power

Elastic band balance

The stretchiness of elastic makes it ideal for using in a home-made weighing balance. The word elastic to a scientist does not only refer to strips or bands of rubber, but anything at all that can be stretched out of shape by pulling it or hanging weights from it. If it goes back to its original shape when the load is removed it is called elastic. Even metal can be elastic when it is in the form of a thin wire or a coiled spring. But even elastic things can snap if you stretch them beyond their elastic limit.

You can make your own elastic band balance that will weigh small objects quite accurately. Find a large, strong elastic band, a screw-in hook (sometimes called a cup hook) or a nail and hammer, a margarine or butter tub and some thin string or strong thread.

The hook needs to be screwed into a suitable wooden board or post so that the elastic band can hang from it. Make holes at four points around the edge of the plastic tub with the point of a pair of scissors and thread pieces of string about 20 cm (8 in) long through the holes, tie them and secure the knots with some sticky tape. Tie the other ends to the bottom of the elastic band so that the tub hangs level. It is also a good idea to pin a piece of paper to the board behind where the tub is hanging.

Using the balance

To use your balance it must first be calibrated. This means that you must mark on the paper the points where the elastic band stretches to when weights are placed in the tub.
If you have some metal weights from some kitchen scales your job will be much easier, but

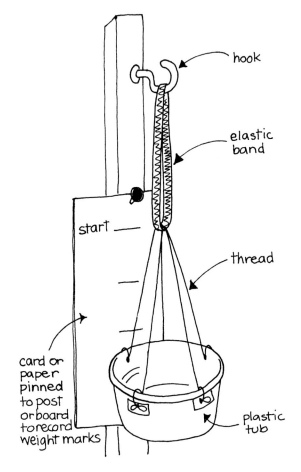

if not you will need to find some packs of sweets or food that show the weight on the side.

Before you begin loading the tub, mark where the knot at the bottom of the band comes on the paper pinned behind it. This is the zero or starting point. Now add a small weight, say 25 grammes and put a mark on the paper next to the knot. Write the weight beside the mark. Do this for every weight or pack that you know the weight of. (Remember that the

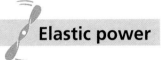

weight shown on food packets means what is inside, not the weight of the pack as well).

You will now have a number of spots on your paper with weights beside them. Can you see a pattern. It is quite possible that weights such as 25, 50, 75 and 100 grammes form a regularly spaced series of spots on the paper. You might even be able to guess where other weights should come on the scale. Draw up your weight scale carefully and then weigh

things that you do not know the weight of. Try a favourite small toy or a few conkers, a large stone or some marbles. Can you read the weight of the objects from your scale?

Although lighter weights will form a regular pattern on your scale, you may notice that heavier weights that really stretch the band do not fit the pattern so well. Be careful not to put in too much weight as this will go beyond the elastic limit and the band will snap.

The power of elastic

When you stretch an elastic band you are storing up energy in the elastic so that when you let go, the band can release that energy as it springs back to its original shape. If the elastic band can be attached to something, energy stored by pulling or twisting the elastic can be used to move the object in some way.

Ping-pong ball launcher

You can fire a table tennis ball right across a room with this elastic band powered launcher. You will need a strong cardboard tube about 40 cm (16 in) long and 5 cm (2 in) across. The kind of tube used inside a roll of cooking foil or plastic wrap would be just right. Whatever you choose, make sure that a table tennis ball can roll through it easily. The firing pin is made from a smaller, shorter tube or cylinder shape that

will fit easily inside the larger one. Something like a 'Smarties' tube or even a piece of broom handle or wooden stick about 15 cm (6 in) long would work well.

Make two small holes with the point of a pair of scissors either side of the tube about 15 cm (6 in) from one end. Push a brass paper fastener through each hole. Put a large elastic band, about 10 cm (4 in) long, over the end stud of both fasteners. Then open up the fasteners inside the tube to hold the bands firmly in place.

If you are using a piece of wood or dowel for the firing pin, knock a nail in either side of one end. If you are using a cardboard tube, make holes in one end with the point of some scissors and push the stub of a pencil, or a short length of garden cane through the holes so that it sticks out about 2 cm (1 in) on either side. Push the smaller tube up inside the larger one and pull the elastic bands back to fit over the nails or pencil ends.

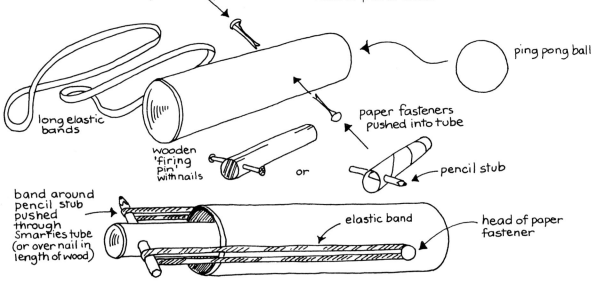

ping pong ball

long elastic bands

wooden 'firing pin' with nails

or

paper fasteners pushed into tube

pencil stub

band around pencil stub pushed through Smarties tube (or over nail in length of wood)

elastic band

head of paper fastener

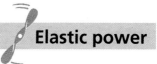

Firing the launcher

To fire your launcher, drop a table tennis ball down the tube. You will need to hold the end up at a slight angle so that the ball doesn't roll out. Pull the firing pin back until it almost reaches the end of the larger tube (be careful not to pull it all the way out) aim carefully and fire. DON'T point your launcher at people, pets or expensive ornaments!

The energy in the stretched elastic pulls the firing pin up into the launch tube and pushes the ball out of the launch tube with great force. Can you think of ways of making your launcher even more powerful? A longer firing pin will stretch the bands even further, or double elastic bands on each side might improve the power, try it and see.

What about the launch angle? For this test you may need to go outside for extra room. Fire a ball with the tube almost level, try again with the tube pointing up at a greater angle and keep repeating your tests with greater and greater launch angles. Is there one angle that propels the ball further than any other? How accurate is your launcher? Put a target on the ground such as a hoop or a large box and see how many times out of ten you can land a ball inside the box or hoop.

Propeller power

When an elastic band is twisted round and round it is also storing energy and when it is released it will untwist rapidly. This release of energy can be used to turn a propeller to push things along. You can buy a small, plastic propeller very cheaply in most good model shops. You may even be lucky enough to be able to buy a propeller kit that contains the wires and elastic as well, but if not, this is what you need. The propeller should have two blades and be about 12 to 15 cm (5 or 6 in) long with a hole drilled through the centre. Ask in a hardware shop for some strong, stiff wire that will pass easily through the hole in the propeller, you will only need a very little.

Using a pair of pliers or wire cutters, cut a piece about 5cm (2 in) long. Bend up 5mm (about 1/4 in) at one end and push it through the propeller. Next thread a round play bead or something similar on the end. The squirter nozzle from a washing up liquid bottle also works well. Finally bend the end of the wire into a hook shape with pliers.

To drive the propeller you will need a long elastic band, a piece of light wood about 30cm (12in) long, 2.5 cm (1 in) wide and 1cm (1/2 in) thick, a small screw hook and a small screw eyelet.

Screw the hook in one end of the length of wood and the eyelet in the other. Push the wire hook-end of the propeller through the eyelet and stretch the elastic band between the propeller hook and hook screwed into the other end of the wood.

Wind up the propeller and let go. It will spin rapidly and you may actually feel the power of the propeller pulling on the wood. You can use your propeller power pack for all kinds of things. Try some of the following ideas.

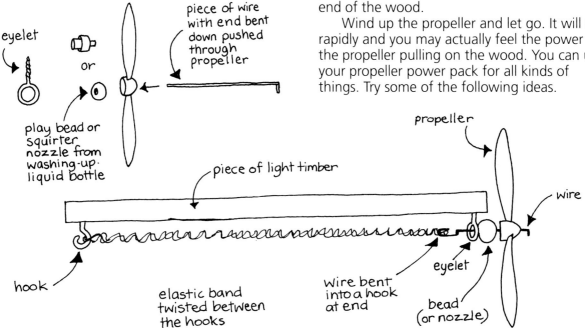

eyelet

or

play bead or squirter nozzle from washing-up. liquid bottle

piece of wire with end bent down pushed through propeller

piece of light timber

hook

elastic band twisted between the hooks

Wire bent into a hook at end

eyelet

bead (or nozzle)

propeller

wire

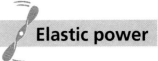

Aerial transport

Stretch a length of nylon fishing line or thin string tightly across a room. Make two loops from some strong, stiff wire that can be hooked over the line at one end and twisted with a pair of pliers around the wood holding the propeller at the other end. Make sure that the wood is held level, and that it is low enough for the propeller to clear the nylon line.

Wind up the propeller so that the band is tight and let go. As the propeller turns it will move the whole power pack along the nylon line, but which way does it go? You may already have discovered that a propeller can push or pull depending on the way it is wound up. Does the propeller push the stick along the line, as though it were at the back, or does it pull from the front? Does the whole transporter move faster when pushed or pulled? The propellers on most aircraft pull the plane through the air, but propellers on ships push them through the water.

Speed boat

Make a simple boat shape from a polystyrene ceiling tile or meat tray. (The kind that many foods sold in supermarkets come wrapped up on). The cabin can be made from a small cardboard box glued to the top of the tray and the propeller power pack can be taped or held in place under the tray with elastic bands. Make sure that the propeller can spin freely.

You will need a wide expanse of water to give your speed boat a good trip. The bath will do, but perhaps a large, deep puddle or a pond might be better. Wind up your propeller and place the tray in the water. As the propeller turns it will push the boat along. If the propeller is half out of the water it may splash quite a lot. Can you think of a way of mounting the propeller mechanism so that it is lower in the water and pushes more powerfully?

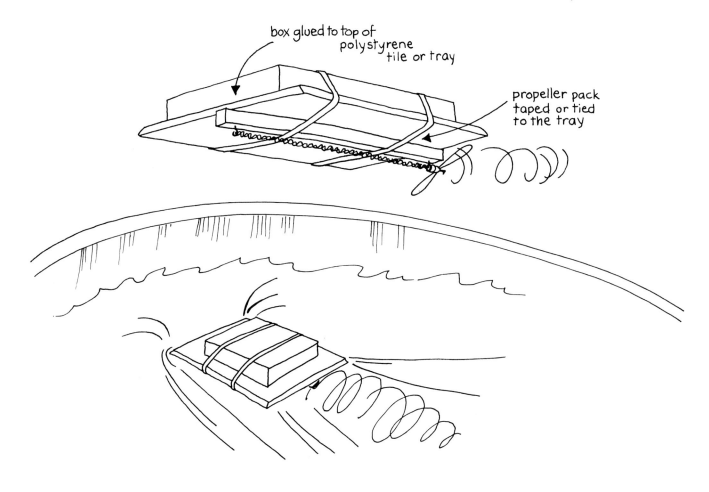

box glued to top of polystyrene tile or tray

propeller pack taped or tied to the tray

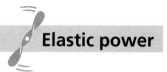

Propeller-driven car

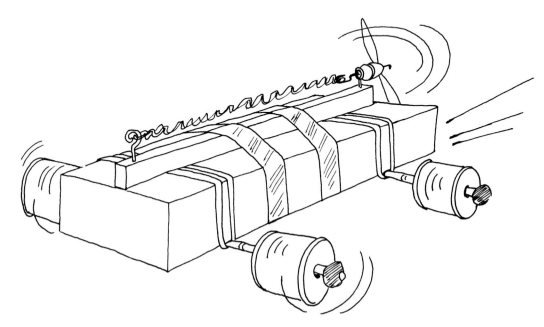

The four-wheeled wagon described earlier (page 50) can be powered by your propeller. Hold the power pack on the top of the wagon with sticky tape, string or elastic bands. Discover whether the wagon moves better when it is pushed or pulled by winding up the propeller first in one direction, then the other. With all propeller driven models it is very important to make them as light as possible to get the most speed and distance from them.

Giant elastic-band crawler

This is based on the well known cotton reel 'tanks' that your parents or grandparents may remember making years ago. Find an empty tin with a removable lid, such as a cocoa tin. Ask an adult to help you knock a hole in the centre of the lid and the base of the tin with a large nail and a hammer.

Push a long elastic band through the bottom of the tin and stop it from pulling back through by pushing a piece of stick or pencil stub through the loop of the elastic band. Hold the pencil stub in place with some sticky tape. Thread the other end of the elastic band through the hole in the lid and push the lid firmly in place. Lastly push the elastic through a play bead and secure it by pushing something like a thin garden cane, pencil or knitting needle about 20cm (8in) long through the loop. Wind up the elastic band by turning the cane, pencil or knitting needle and lay the tin on a flat surface. As the elastic band unwinds the end of the stick pushes against the ground and

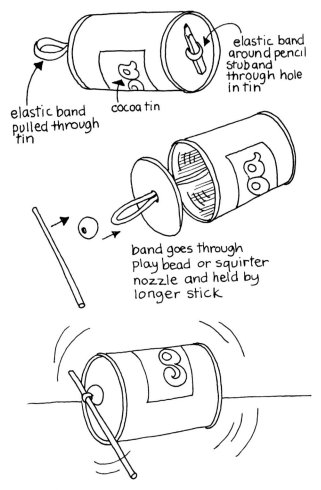

elastic band around pencil stub and through hole in tin

elastic band pulled through tin

cocoa tin

band goes through play bead or squirter nozzle and held by longer stick

the tin crawls along. If the surface is too smooth the tin might slip so try a carpeted area or level grass. Wide rubber bands round the edges of the tin will act like tyres and give better grip. Once you have got your crawler working well , discover how powerful it is. Try getting it to crawl up a slope. How high can you tilt the board before your crawler can no longer move up it?

Stretching things too far

The strength of different materials such as fabrics, fibres, plastics and even human hair can be measured by stretching them to their limit. In this investigation you can discover the strongest plastic used in a range of shopping bags.

When scientists and engineers run tests on things they take great care to make the test as fair as possible. One way of doing this is to make sure that the conditions for each test are exactly the same. For example, if you are going to test plastics you must use the same sized piece each time and set it up and load it in the same way. In this way the only differences should be in the actual strength of each piece. To set up the investigation you will need to get a number of different plastic bags such as those used to wrap or carry food in shops and supermarkets. Using a pair of scissors, cut a strip from each one that is exactly 20cm (8in) long and 1cm (0.4in) wide. Make sure that you note which strip comes from which bag.

Firmly tie a piece of strong thread or string to the top of the plastic strip and another to the bottom. Use the top string to tie the strip to a nail or hook, or tie it around a stick lying between two chairs. Tie the bottom string to the handle of a bucket or similar container.

Begin to fill the bucket slowly with stones or soil, sand or even water. It is a good idea to set up your test so that the bucket is only a few centimetres from the ground. In this way, when the strip snaps the bucket will not have far to fall. Keep adding more weight slowly and carefully, watching the plastic strip all the time. You will see it stretch and change shape until, finally, it rips and pulls apart. KEEP YOUR TOES WELL OUT OF THE WAY.

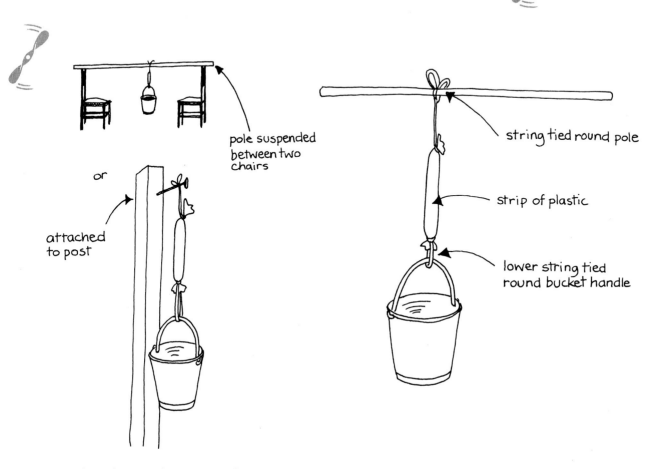

pole suspended
between two
chairs

or

attached
to post

string tied round pole

strip of plastic

lower string tied
round bucket handle

When the strip has snapped weigh the bucket and its contents on some bathroom scales. If you are using water as the weight, be careful not to spill any. Make a note of which bag the strip came from and the amount of weight needed to snap it. Repeat your test in exactly the same way for the other strips and make a record of each result. From your notes you will be able to recommend the strongest bags as well as those to avoid.

If this form of testing interests you, see if you can set up something similar to test a thread pulled from a piece of fabric or even a single human hair. You probably won't need a bucket, but a large, plastic tub hanging from the hair may work very well. Be prepared to have lots of small weights standing by because a hair can actually support far more weight than you might think possible.

See if you can discover who in your family has the strongest hair. Is a black hair stronger than a blond hair? Do red heads have the strongest hair of all? Also, if you mark the starting point at the bottom of the hair, then load slowly and gently with small increases in weight, you can discover how far a human hair will stretch before breaking.